COLD WAR COLORING

POLITICAL ADULT COLORING BOOKS OF THE KENNEDY ERA

COMPILED BY ABOUT COMICS

A PRESIDENTIAL BOOKSHELF™ PROJECT

ABOUT COMICS | CAMARILLO, CALIFORNIA

DEDICATION

To the libraries, collectors, and used book sellers
who help store and make available the vast history
of literature in all its forms.

Special thanks go to Kathy Burkhart of Gebhard
and Burkhart Books and to Lynne Haims of Ground
Zero Books, whose efforts above and beyond the
call of duty helped make this book possible.

◇◇

JFK Coloring Book originally published by Kanrom, Inc., May, 1962.

New Frontier Comic Coloring Book originally published by Arthur J. Weaver, July, 1962.

Nikita Sergeyevich Khrushchev Coloring Book originally published by Co-Existence Press, 1962.

Khrushchev's Top Secret Coloring Book orignally published by Universal Publishing and Distributing
Corporation, November, 1962.

The John Birch Coloring Book originally published by The Serious Products Company, August, 1962.

Annotations created for this edition by About Comics.
Compilation copyright 2016 About Comics.

ISBN: 978-1936404-62-9
Published April, 2016.

For bulk orders, custom covers, or other inquiries, contact *questions@aboutcomics.com*

CONTENTS

FOREWORD

With America in the throes of an adult coloring book craze, it's easy to overlook that we've had such a craze before, in the early 1960s. However, the adult coloring books of the time were very different. They were not meant to be colored for a pastime or as therapy. Indeed, they were not meant to be colored at all (although sometimes they got colored nonetheless.) Instead, these books used a parody of the coloring book form in order to cast comment on society, on politics, on careers, and on hobbies.

The very first adult coloring book was *Executive Coloring Book*, a look at thew New York men in their grey flannel suits and the numb lifestyles they lead. When that book was released in December of 1961, it rushed onto the best seller lists. The form turned political with *JFK Coloring Book* just five months later, quick enough that the creators of the new book claiming that it was coincidental and already in the works before *Executive* was released could be believed. More political parodies followed, some goofy, others acidic.

During the Kennedy administration, there were a fair number of such political coloring books issued (the contents of this book is only a sampling of them, and does not include such examples as *The Senator's Coloring Book* or *The Dis-UNited Nations Coloring Book*, among others.) The form was already dying down before Kennedy was assassinated, but it did not disappear completely. There are still occasional forays into political coloring books, with the 2016 election cycle bringing several different Donald Trump-themed coloring books. Hillary Clinton coloring books, a coloring book of a partially clothed and curiously beefcake Bernie Sanders, and more. Even some of the original hands remain involved, as Dennis M. Altman (one of the authors of *Executive* and whom you'll find represented in these pages in *The John Birch Coloring Book*) has relatively recently released *The Choke Brothers Coloring Book*, his take on the poweful conservative Koch brothers.

So here's a little piece of history for you. It's easy reading, with lots of pictures. And if you want to get out your crayons, that's up to you!

Nat Gertler
Publisher
About Comics
June, 2016

COLORING BOOK

Inspiration: R. Nixon

Conception: Alexander A. Roman

Drawings: Mort Drucker

Copy: Paul Laikin

and

(Man, like if the Prez doesn't dig

this bit, I don't want to be in

this alone.)

Jackie Kannon

Nineteen sixty-two's *JFK Coloring Book* was the most successful adult coloring book of the decade, landing on the *New York Times* non-fiction best seller list for 14 weeks. It also helped launch the upbeat mocking of the Kennedy clan, coming out before Vaughn Meader's popular comedy album *The First Family*. Sales of the book had already been petering out for a while before the 1963 assassination of President Kennedy, which was the end of any market for this volume. (It remained out of print until About Comics, the publisher of this book, returned it to press in 2014.) The publisher would claim that the book was already in development before the *Executive Coloring Book* saw print.

The main creative team of this book, writer Paul Laikin and artist Mort Drucker (both regulars in the pages of the humor magazine *Mad*) would return to the coloring book form in the 1980s, producing satires of then-President Ronald Reagan and Ollie North, key figure in the Iran-Contra scandal.

This is my Daddy.
He has a good job.
He works for the Government.
Color him red, white and blue.
My daddy is very important.
He has a lot of people working for him.
They would do anything for my daddy.
Color their noses burnt umber.

7

This is my Mommy.
She is very beautiful.
She is the most beautiful Mommy ever.
Color her beautiful.
See her pretty clothes?
They are very expensive.
They cost my daddy a lot of money.
Is that why he can't afford an overcoat?

See the pretty White House?
It is my pretty White House.
I live here.
Color it pretty white.
Better hurry up and color it.
Mommy is doing a lot of redecorating.
If you wait too long
You may have to color it Chartreuse.

See the funny chair?
It is daddy's funny chair.
It is a Rocking chair.
Daddy sits on it and rocks.
Rock, Rock, Rock.
My daddy loves his rocking chair.
My daddy is always sitting on it.
Daddy doesn't like to be off his rocker.

This is my Uncle.
See how young he is?
Color him green.
When he grows up he will get Daddy's job.
People say that he gives daddy orders.
I don't think daddy takes orders from him.
My daddy doesn't take orders from anybody.
Just Mommy.

See the nice man?
He is my other uncle.
Doesn't he look like Daddy?
Color him the same.
He is next in line for Daddy's job.
Now he is learning the business.
He will start at the bottom.
He will be in Congress.

This is my Brother.
He is only a baby.
He will have to wait until 1996.
To get Daddy's job.
I am older than my Brother.
I will get the job in 1992.
Isn't it fun to play this game?
Isn't it fun to play Monopoly?

13

What is the Supreme Court?
Daddy says it will look like this one day.
Wouldn't that be fun?
You would never get mixed up.
There are ten men here.
Count them ----Ten.
Daddy wants more people working.
Daddy loves everybody.

See the pretty lady?
She is my Aunt.
She is mommy's sister.
She says she's a Princess.
Where is her crown?
Where is her magic wand?
Is she really a Princess?
Do you think it's only a Fairy Tale?

See the handsome man?
He is my uncle too.
He is in show business.
He can sing and he can dance.
My aunt must have liked his song and dance.
But he will never get Daddy's job.
He belongs to another clan.
They have their own government.

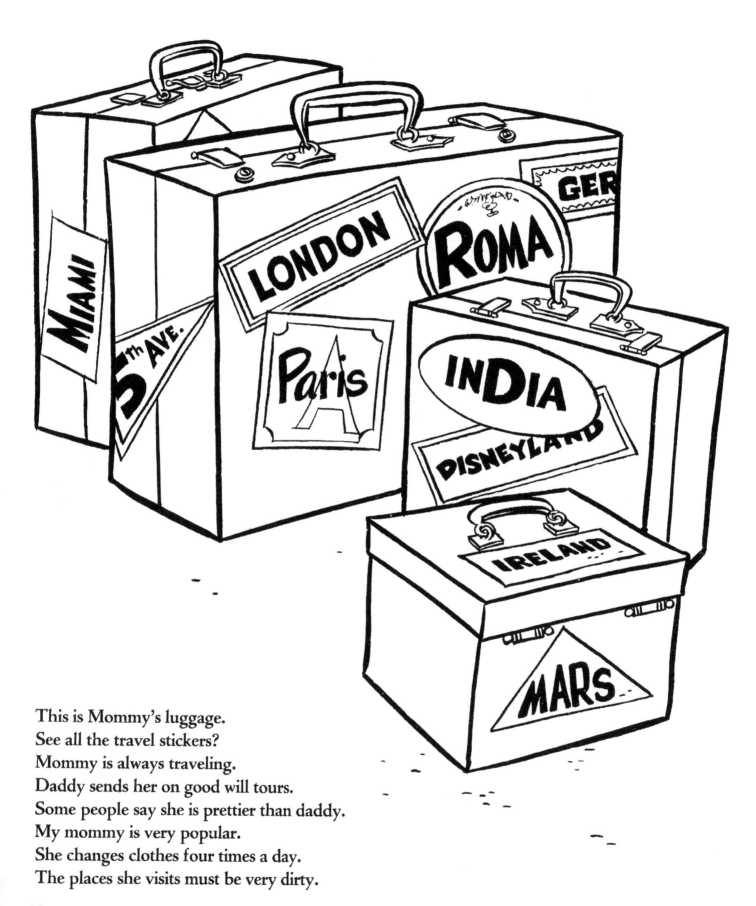

This is Mommy's luggage.
See all the travel stickers?
Mommy is always traveling.
Daddy sends her on good will tours.
Some people say she is prettier than daddy.
My mommy is very popular.
She changes clothes four times a day.
The places she visits must be very dirty.

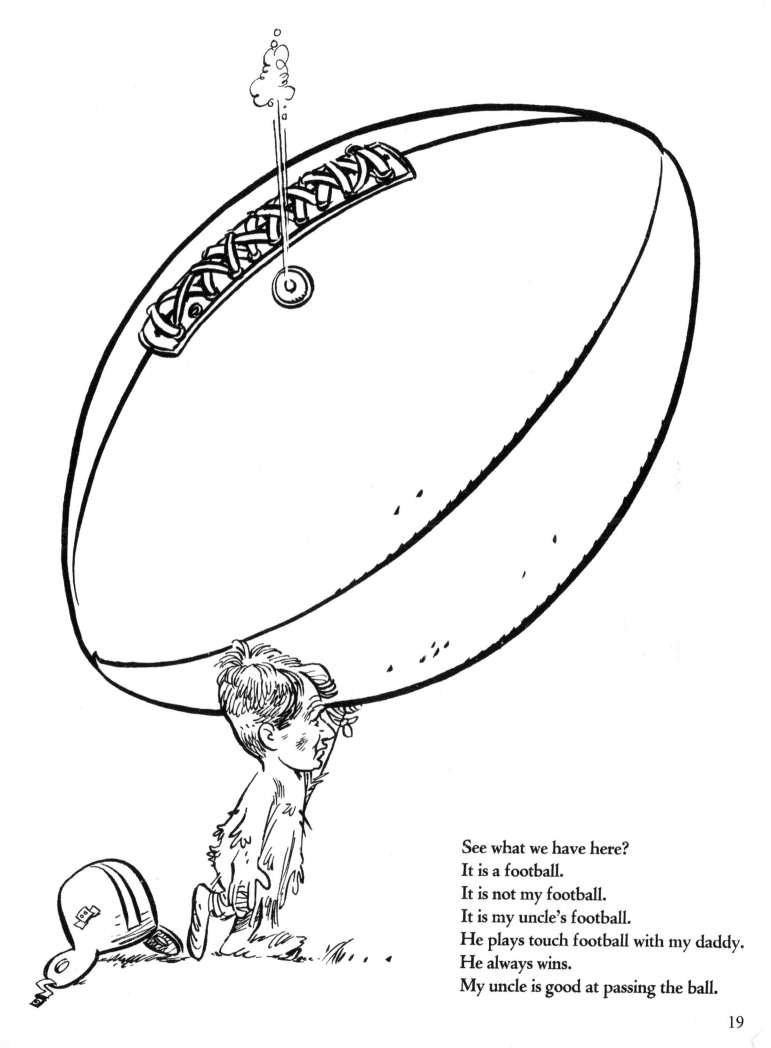

See what we have here?
It is a football.
It is not my football.
It is my uncle's football.
He plays touch football with my daddy.
He always wins.
My uncle is good at passing the ball.

19

Say hello to the fat jolly man.
Hello fat jolly man.
How are you today?
Will you give me another lollipop?
I didn't eat the last one you gave me.
Daddy told me not to.
Why didn't daddy want me to eat it?
Why did he make my doggie taste it first?

Look at all these people.
They are friends of the family.
They are always at our house.
They are very important.
Color them important.
I know almost everybody here.
Just that skinny one in the middle.
I wonder who he is?

21

See the cap and gown?
It is daddy's cap and gown.
Daddy went to Harvard.
Rah, Rah, Rah.
My daddy is very smart.
He used to work hard for his Professors.
Now his Professors work hard for him.
I told you my Daddy was smart!

See the nice man?
Say goodbye to him.
Goodbye nice man!
He is going away.
He is going on a nice long trip.
He will be away for a long time.
He will be the first man on the moon.
My family is sending him.

23

This is daddy's barber.
He is a man.
He is very poor.
He can't even make a living.
All year 'round.
Daddy never takes a haircut.

See the nice boat?
It is a yacht.
A yacht is a rich man's boat.
My daddy has two yachts.
My daddy goes on fishing trips.
My daddy always catches something.
My daddy has a good line.

See the man in the big hat?
He is daddy's helper.
He is very rich.
He comes from Texas.
He has a lot of oil wells.
He owns a big ranch.
He raises cattle.
He raises horses.
He raises lady birds.

This is Daddy's secretary.
He has a good job.
He tells people what daddy said.
He makes a lot of money.
Do you think that is fair?
I don't think that it is fair.
I tell people what Daddy said.
I get a licking.

27

This is the end.
It is the end of this book.
It is also the end of me.
Daddy has just seen this book.
Daddy says I talk too much.
Daddy says I tell too many secrets.
Daddy says I am too candid.
Daddy says I will never be a Politician.

New Frontier
COMIC COLORING BOOK

While *JFK Coloring Book* has the snide humor of a late night talk show host, *New Frontier Comic Coloring Book* has more the harsh political mockery of a right-wing radio show. The book was produced by Arthur J. Weaver Jr., who was not only the grandson of a Republican U.S. congressman and the son of a one-term Republican governor of Nebraska, but ran for the governership himself, failing to get the Republican nomination in 1946.

One interesting aspect of the visuals of this coloring book is that some of the same caricatures are reused, copying and pasting the same figure into different scenes.

As an example of how quickly filled the adult satirical coloring book market was, note that *New Frontier Comic Coloring Book* is not to be confused with the separate, also anti-Kennedy *The New Frontier Coloring Book* put out three months earlier by aircraft engineer Joe B. Nation.

There is no question -- They know best.
Color -- egghead color.

"Medicare will not affect the quality of medicine" -- what a relief.
Color us BUREAUCRATIC.

Congress is holding its own. Maybe at the next session you can get out.

Color -- freedom skidoo.

Honest and truly?
Color everything doubtful.

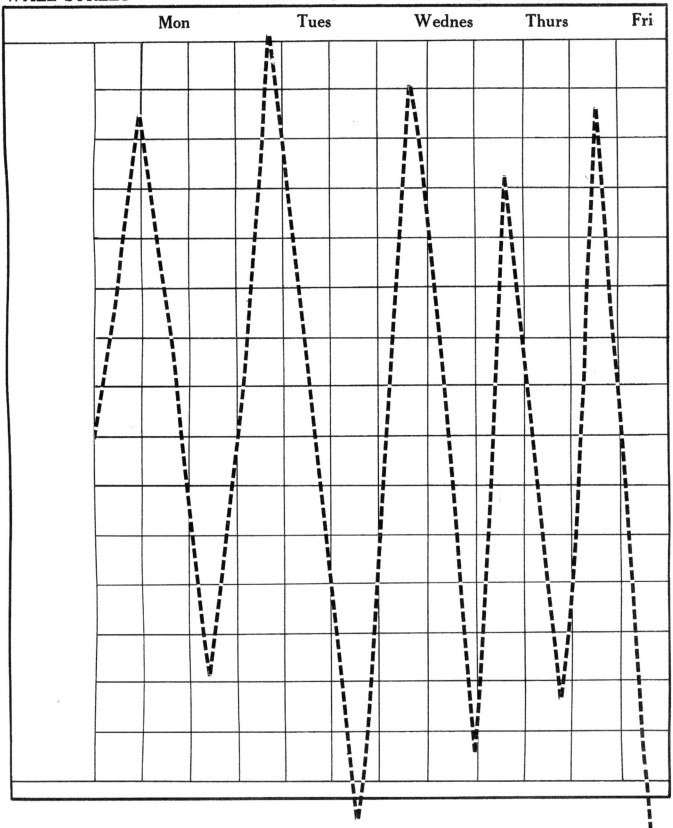

Mon   Tues   Wednes   Thurs   Fri

People really have confidence.
Color me I've lost my shirt.

We couldn't get him, but we could get General Electric and Westinghouse. Color him pretty.

Remember, touch football only. Don't hurt a future president.
Color us — we-don't-need-any-more-quarterbacks color.

Daddy, what's an S.O.B.?
Color her bewildered.

I wish that picture was at the bottom of a grain elevator.
Color him anhydrous.

I shore got powerful friends.
Color him thankful.

I wonder.
Color him clever.

This plus my successful business ventures.
Color him successful.

Daddy, what does "sacrifice" mean?
Color -- sacrificial.

But that isn't enough to buy mama a new girdle.
Color -- Mama-will-be-unhappy color.

Far fetched?
Color them socialized.

Our state department's ace trouble-shooter.
Color -- I-oughta-stay-home-color.

Politics?
Color them a Federal Judge color.

Then we'll all be so happy.
Color -- a Pollyanna color.

Tsk, tsk -- temper, temper.
Color raging purple.

Poolsmanship is the art of practicing diplomacy and not falling in the swimming pool at the same time. **Color us all wet.**

"Victory" is a nasty word.
Color -- a timid color.

Mr. Chairman, just a minute, please -- there is another side.
Color him — don't-confuse-me-with-the-facts color.

Court Of Last Resort.

Color -- What-do-we-do-now color.

That will also take care of election years '64 - '68 - '72 - '76 ad infinitum. Color us smart.

Where did it all go?
Color -- green.

Wrong. Wrong. Wrong.
Color striped -- like State Department pants.

You're right -- you don't understand!
Color him muddled.

That man knows what he is talking about.
Color him a small grain color.

"Medicare will not lead to socialized medicine" -- we are happy about that.
Color us antiseptic.

My brother played no favorites. I was the best qualified.
Color me I-have-to-study-to-keep-up-with-my-class color.

Congress has not gone completely mad yet.
Color a Frankenstein color.

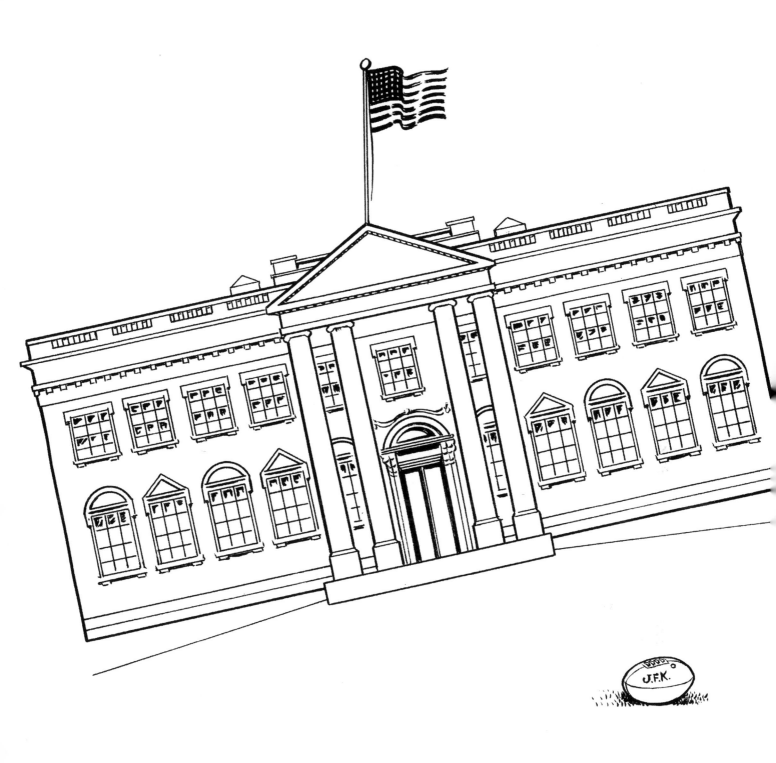

The White House tilts this way because most people in it lean to the left. Color house a left-leaning color.

For
Billie Sol Estes --
with appreciation
and warm
regards --
J.F.K

This is the ever-lovin'

END

Nikita Khrushchev was a colorful figure, so it comes as little surprise that he was also a to-be-colored figure. By the time this coloring book was published in 1962, he had been serving as the Soviet Union's Communist Party secretary since 1953 and as the Premier since 1958; both of these jobs would come to a halt in 1964 when he lost favor, but in 1962 he was riding high. He'd already visited the United States twice, the first time including an attempted visit to Disneyland (scuttled for security reasons), the second time including an incident at the UN where he supposedly used his shoe as a gavel to gain attention during a speech. The Soviet influence was spreading (much to US dismay), and Khrushchev was a powerful symbol for the conflict the world faced.

Writer Amram Ducovny penned a number of humor books and non-fiction books and at least one produced play, but would not achieve his goal of being a published novelist until 2000, at the age of 73. Ducovny's most recognized production is actually his son, *X-Files* star David Duchovny.

NIKITA SERGEYEVICH KHRUSHCHEV COLORING BOOK

by Amram Ducovny
  Co-author of the Psychiatric Coloring
  Book. Co-author (with Fyodor Dostoyevski)
  of the soon-to-be-issued Brothers Karamazov
  Coloring Book.

Dedicated to Nikita Sergeyevich Khrushchev,
without whom this book could not have been
written.

Sub-dedicated to Johann Gutenberg, without
whom this book could not have been printed.

Really dedicated to world peace, without which
there will be no more whom.

Drawings by Ken Nunes and Adrien Prober

My name is Nikita Sergeyevich Khrushchev.

This is my coloring book.

What is your name?

What country do you own?

Do you need technical aid?
    ballet dancers?
    military advisors?

Just dial KRemlin 1-1111

    no waiting
    absolutely no security

    Easy five-year plans arranged.

I am Nikita Sergeyevich Khrushchev. Color me red. If you are
an American imperialist, color me red, white and blue. If you
are a neutral, color yourself red.

This is my home. It is cold and drafty. I like to go on
trips. Color and disguise me so I can sneak into Disneyland.

These are the people who make the laws in my country. They are all very intelligent. They always agree with me. Color them healthy as long as they agree with me.

This is my Berlin Wall. It keeps bad, starving West Germans away from good, well-fed East Germans. The West Germans are all Nazis. The East Germans were all born after World War II.

This is me and my wife on a double date with another couple.
He always wants to talk politics. I want to talk to his wife.
Color me green.

This is one of my top conscientious, dedicated agents.
Take a Birch branch and smear him red.

These are some of my far-away friends. They are devoted
Communists, dedicated to stamping out religion. Color them
intelligent and hungry.

This is an American nuclear test. It contaminates the world with radiation. Color it black.

This is a Russian experiment in the peaceful uses of nuclear energy. There is no fall-out. Color it white.

This is an American astronaut being launched for the moon to set up a military base. He will fail. Color him bloody.

This is a Russian cosmonaut going to the moon to start an agricultural farm. He will succeed. Color him corny.

This is me leaving for a vacation in Cuba. Cuba has a wonderful climate. Many Russians, Chinese and American intelligence agents spend their holidays there.

I like to relax with my shoes off. Bring me my pipe and slippers
and color me contented.

This is an Englishman named Macmillan. He is always coming
to see me. He says we must co-exist. I say I am always ready
to co-exist as long as I get my own way. Color him unreasonable.

This is a man who always talks about me but never wants to see me. Why does he hate me? Why doesn't he send me French postcards? Color him 18th century royal blue.

This is a tomb of my friend, Nikolai Lenin. He used to share it with a man named Stalin. But my country's economy is so good he now has it all to himself.

This is my laundry man. I taught him to be a Marxist. Now he
is trying to teach me to be a Marxist. He burns my—shirtcuffs.

This is a little girl. I like this little girl. I send her
presents. She sends them back. She says her daddy is very rich
and she doesn't need presents. Color her a misguided victim of the
capitalist conspiracy.

I met this man in a kitchen. What is a man doing in a kitchen?
Color him shocking pink.

This is the worst man in West Germany. He is 86 years old.
No politician in my country lives that long. Color him obsolete.

There is a Russian invention. My country invented everything.
We are a very inventive and modest people.

There is such prosperity in my country that everyone can afford to dress casually. I brought this style back from my visit to Hollywood. Color them loud.

These are the women of my country. They are hard workers. They
are not skinny like the starved capitalistic women. I love the
women of my country. Why doesn't De Gaulle invite me to France?

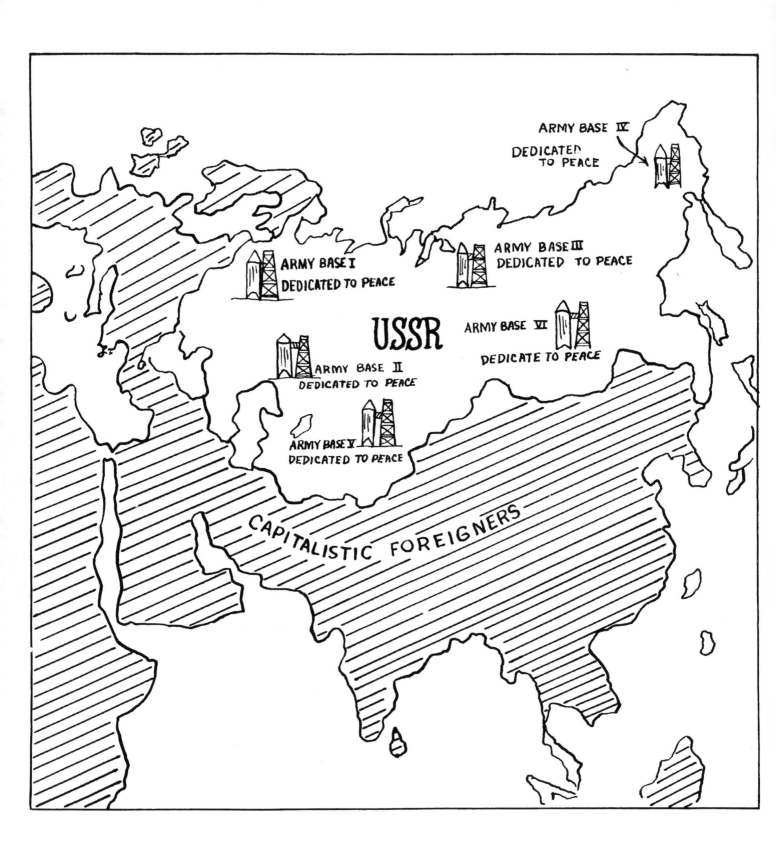

This is my country. Wouldn't you too like to see it? Just phone CIA 1-4000 and ask for Mr. Powers. Remember, half the fun is not getting there.

KHRUSHCHEV'S
TOP SECRET
COLORING BOOK
YOUR FIRST RED READER

ONE DOLLAR
(2 RUBLES)

KHRUSHCHEV

COLORING BOOK

[By Appointment to H. R. H. Czar Nicholas II]

Conceived and Written by

GENE SHALIT

Drawings by

JACK DAVIS

Courageous Publisher

ARNOLD E. ABRAMSON

Vice Commissar For Forced Sales

ROBERT J. ABRAMSON

Art Commissar

FRANC L. ROGGERI

Banned in

BULGARIA, RUMANIA, ALBANIA, ESTONIA, LAVIA, LITHUANIA,

HUNGARIA, CUBIA, SIBERIA, and SHMETINIA

Dropped into Russia by

KABLE NEWS COMPANY U-2 PLANES

November, 1962 brought another coloring book focused on Khrushchev, this one writted by Gene Shalit and illustrated another of the great caricaturists from the pages of *Mad*, Jack Davis. The Soviet premiere proved such a rich topic that at least one other coloring book was produced, *Sing Along with Khrushchev*.

This is my mother. This is my father.
There are my three sisters. Here are
my brothers. See my neighbors. See
their six children. See my other
neighbors. See their children. What
a big group we are! We all live in
the same room.

See our family.
We are going to spend our vacation
at my Grandmother's.
How we are looking forward to it!
My Grandmother lives in our cellar.

VULGER BOATMAN

See our radio.
It has such a big dial.
How many numbers it has!
How come it gets only one station?

This is the Moscow Stadium.
The teams are playing for the soccer championship.
Today we are playing Albania.
We do not care if we win or lose.
What counts is sportsmanship.
Color the Albanian's skull red.

This is the courtroom in our village.
See the jury.
See the judge.
They have heard all the evidence.
The case is complete.
But they have not given their verdict.
They are waiting for the messenger to
come with the envelope from Moscow.

99

There is the Press Secretary of the USA.
He is skeet shooting with our Leader.
The Press Secretary is very smart.
He does not let our Leader get behind him.

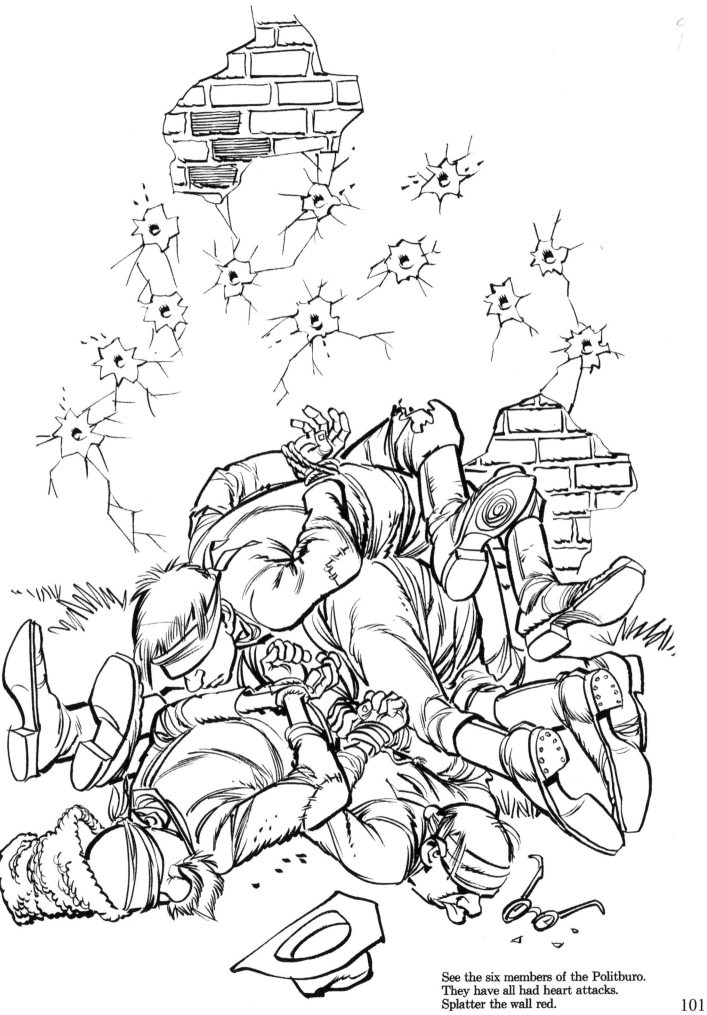

See the six members of the Politburo.
They have all had heart attacks.
Splatter the wall red.

See our glorious amateur athletes.
They are preparing for the Olympics.
How happy they are!
They are well paid.

See our glorious inventors.
That man is inventing the telephone.
The other man is inventing the wheel.
See the third man.
He is waiting for our embassy in Washington
to send in this week's patents.

See the Great Banquet Hall of the Kremlin.
We are honoring our glorious Chinese allies.
They are studying the menu.
They can't decide between list A and list B.
How friendly everyone is.
Hail to the peace-loving peoples' democracies!
Only one glorious ally is not in this room.

We could never have a banquet without him.

He ... is ... in ... the ....

.... kitchen.

See the big hole.
It is fourteen miles wide and seven miles deep.
It was Kievograd.
Our underground atomic scientists miscalculated.
Color their faces red.

This is our collective farm.
We grow corn.
Our leader visited us last week.
Next year there will be more corn to eat.
After he left there were fewer people.

108

See the donkey.
Hello, donkey.
He works in the fields.
He is seventeen years old.
His name is "Tractor."
We have more tractors than
any other country in the world.

109

Our collective has a library.
It has many history books.
They faithfully record the past events
of our glorious country.
I wonder why our history books are loose leaf.

Here are members of our glorious diplomatic corps.
They will go to many countries as peaceful
envoys of the people.
They have all graduated from spy school.

111

This is a line.
Our glorious country is filled with lines.
Some lines are for stores.
Some are for Lenin's tomb.
We have been standing in this line for three hours.
I wonder what this line is for.

How happy my father is!
Mother has just had a baby.
We have not seen our new baby yet.
We will see it when our mother comes in
from ploughing the fields.

113

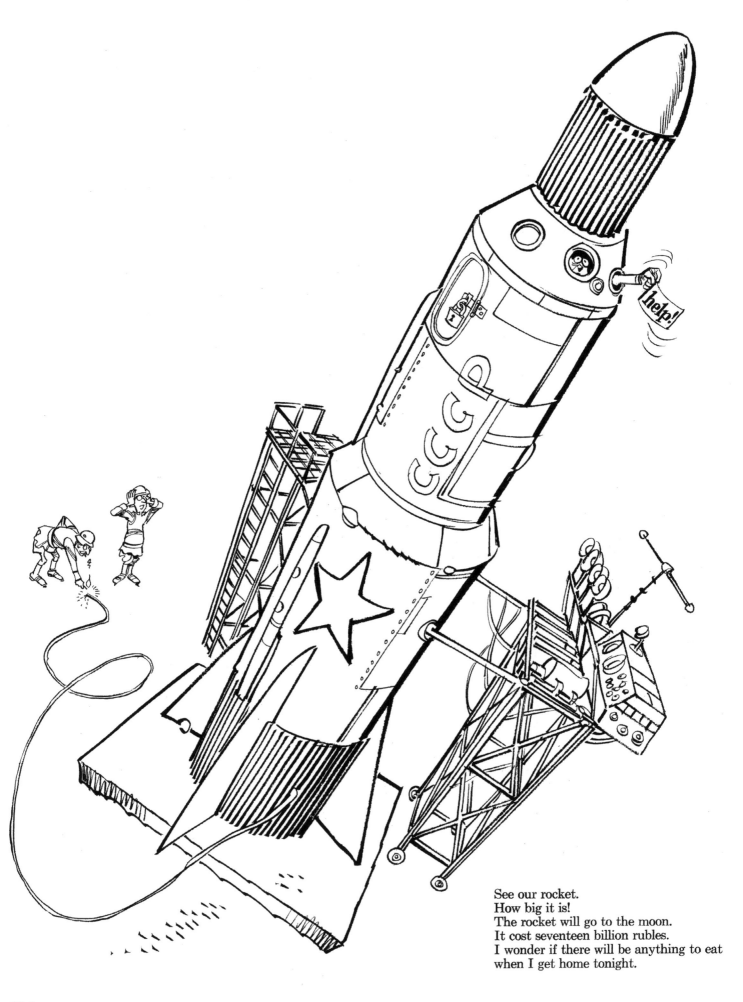

See our rocket.
How big it is!
The rocket will go to the moon.
It cost seventeen billion rubles.
I wonder if there will be anything to eat
when I get home tonight.

This is the document room in the Kremlin.
Our treaties are written here.
See our Director of Treaties.
He has won the Order of Lenin.
He invented disappearing ink.

See our leader.
He is leaving for the United Nations.
He will be there three weeks.
He is taking one suit.
He is taking one shirt.
He is taking three shoes.
Two are for wearing.
One is for pounding.

THE JOHN BIRCH COLORING BOOK

(NOT APPROVED BY THE JOHN BIRCH SOCIETY)

The adult coloring book craze of the 1960s was launched not with a political coloring book but with more of a social commentary. The *Executive Coloring Book*, published by The Funny Products Company, launched in December, 1961 and flew onto the *New York Times* best-sellers chart.

The next year, two-thirds of the team that crafted that book did enter the political realm with *The John Birch Coloring Book*. Published this time by The Serious Products Company, this coloring book attempted to skewer the John Birch Society, a conservative group which had grown greatly since its 1958 launch. Often seen as a paranoid group that saw One World Government in every example of international cooperation and Communists in every government program, the group wielded its greatest influence in the 1960s. While they still exist, they are no longer seen as having an impact on the larger conversation.

"To the rear, march!"

**General Edwin A. Walker,
West Point, 1931**

THE JOHN BIRCH COLORING BOOK
(A blue book)

Title No. 10515

by **MARTIN A. COHEN**
(of EXECUTIVE COLORING BOOK fame)
DENNIS M. ALTMAN
(of EXECUTIVE COLORING BOOK fame)
ROBERT E. NATKIN
(of no fame at all)

This book is respectfully dedicated to Dwight D. Eisenhower, and to the many other loyal Americans who have been maligned by extremist groups.

THIS IS OUR EAGLE. We cut off his left wing. Now he is an All American eagle. But he only flies in circles.

THIS IS OUR FOUNDER. He had a bright new idea.

THESE ARE MY CRAYONS. I use them a lot. Color them scarlet, crimson, red and pinko.

THIS IS MY NEWSPAPER. I like to keep up.

THIS IS MY PSYCHIATRIST. I go to him whenever I feel my mind beginning to open.

THIS IS WHERE I STAND. See how right I am? If I move any

farther to the right, I will fall off the world (which is flat).

**I AM A
RUGGED
INDIVIDUALIST.**
I think for myself.

Me too.

Same here.

Ditto.   **Check.**   **Right.**

THIS IS OUR CLOCK. It says tock-tick, tock-tick, tock-tick . . .

THIS IS OUR ELECTRONIC BRAIN. It tells you the
answers before it gets the facts.

THIS IS R. HOOD. He was a thief. He stole from the rich and gave to the poor. Just like income tax.

WHAT KIND OF CLUB IS THIS? No pool. No golf course.
And they let foreigners in.

THIS IS OUR NEIGHBORHOOD OBSERVATION CENTER.

We just like to keep in touch.

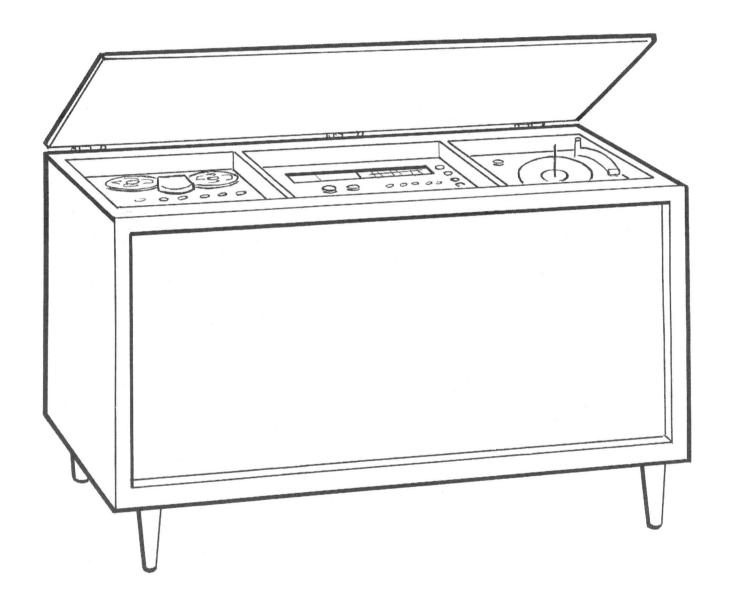

THIS IS MY STEREO. Both speakers are on the right.

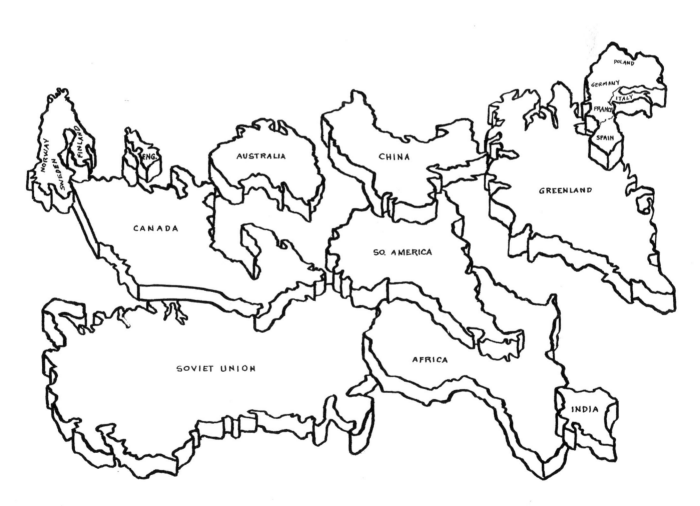

THIS IS THE WORLD. It is made of two parts: America and un-America.

THIS IS MY SWEETHEART. She never changes. Not even her socks.

BEWARE OF THIS MAN. He is a conscious, dedicated agent of the international communist conspiracy.

HOW MANY COMMUNISTS CAN YOU FIND IN THIS PICTURE?
I can find eleven. It takes practice.

THESE ARE OUR LABELS. They are very sticky. They are easy to put on. They are hard to take off.

**SEE? SEE? SEE? LOOK! There's one!
They're everywhere! Quick, get him!**

THIS IS AN EGGHEAD. Remember what we did to him?

Remember when Un-American Activities Committees did more than just talk? Those were the good old days.

I pledge allegiance to the flag of the United States of America, and to the Re= public for which it stands; one nation, indivisible, with liberty and justice for ~~all~~. some

145

●

This innocent-looking black dot is a minia-
ture, self-powered, transistorized, highly
sensitive, long-range radio transmitter
(made in U.S.A.). We have been listening to
you while you were reading this book. Too
bad if you laughed.

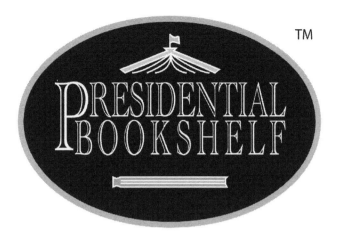

The **Presidenial Bookshelf** project is designed to reflect on the American presidency from a wide variety of angles, whether ithrough the eyes of children, from the sharp pen of satirists, or from the words of the Presidents themselves. Books in this project are available at museum, presidential library, and national park gift shops, as well as online.

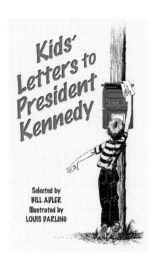

Kid's Letters to President Kennedy
From the early days of the JFK administration comes this collection of letters from the youth of America, edited by Bill Adler (creator of the *New York Times* best=seller *The Kennedy Wit*, profusely illustrated by Silent Spring artist Louis Darling.
ISBN 978-1936404-61-2

Dear President Johnson reveals children's
letters to LBJ, edited by *New York Times* best=seller Bill Adler, illustrated by Peanuts creator Charles M. Schulz.
ISBN 978-1936404-56-8

Find these books and more at
www.PresidentialBookshelf.com

LOOK FOR
ADULT COLORING BOOKS OF THE 1960S
WHERE YOU GOT THIS BOOK!
FROM ABOUT COMICS

Made in the USA
Middletown, DE
02 December 2016